BEGINNER'S LUCK

U.A. Fanthorpe (1929-2009) was born in Kent and read English at St Anne's College, Oxford, before training as a teacher. She was Head of English at Cheltenham Ladies' College, and then became 'a middle-aged drop-out' in order to write, publishing her first collection, *Side Effects*, in 1978. Her eight volumes of poetry were all published by Peterloo, and her *Selected Poems* was published by Penguin in 1986. Her 1995 collection *Safe as Houses* was included on the A-level syllabus. Enitharmon Press published her *Christmas Poems* (2002) and *From Me to You* (2007), love poems by Fanthorpe and R.V. Bailey.

In 1994 U.A. Fanthorpe was the first woman to be nominated for the post of Oxford Professor of Poetry. She was made a CBE in 2001 and given the Queen's Gold Medal for Poetry in 2003, when her *Collected Poems* was published.

Her *New and Collected Poems* (2010) and *Berowne's Book* (2015) were both published by Enitharmon. Some of her early, un-collected poems are now included in *Beginner's Luck*, edited by R.V. Bailey, published by Bloodaxe in 2019.

U.A. FANTHORPE

Beginner's Luck

EDITED BY
R.V. BAILEY

BLOODAXE BOOKS

ISBN: 978 1 78037 474 1

First published 2019 by
Bloodaxe Books Ltd,
Eastburn,
South Park,
Hexham,
Northumberland NE46 1BS.

www.bloodaxebooks.com
For further information about Bloodaxe titles
please visit our website and join our mailing list
or write to the above address for a catalogue

Supported using public funding by
**ARTS COUNCIL
ENGLAND**

Cover design: Neil Astley & Pamela Robertson-Pearce.

Printed in Great Britain by Bell & Bain Limited, Glasgow, Scotland, on
acid-free paper sourced from mills with FSC chain of custody certification.

CONTENTS

INTRODUCTION

These poems were written mostly in the mid-1970s, before (1983) U.A. Fanthorpe briefly escaped from being a hospital receptionist and became, for a couple of years, Arts Council Writer Fellow at St Martin's College in Lancaster, where she experienced the heady situation of being paid a salary for writing poems.

These are the first serious moves in a demanding game, and I daresay she may well have been horrified that they should be exposed to human gaze. In the unthinking chaos of a poet's daily life, for thirty years or more, in Waitrose plastic bags along with all sorts of other miscellaneous rubbish, such papers were tossed annually into the attic. It has taken seven years to run them all to earth (let alone, in some cases, to read the writing). They are the infant poems that lie behind the mature preoccupations of *Consequences* and *Safe as Houses*, behind 'Rising Damp' (and even behind those affectionately popular poems 'BC: AD' and 'Atlas'). In these poems, the originality, the freshness (even the rashness) of the language, and of the poet's point of view make cautious steps into the daylight.

My original intention was to select from the three hundred or so unpublished poems only the "better" poems, the longer poems that dealt with serious subjects in respectable formal cadences. But such a scenario was doomed from the start. Fanthorpe's poems don't lie down and behave in such a suburban manner, and they refused to fall into line with such a bloodless approach. So this selection is a sort of dog's dinner of the early artless, the experimental, and what reviewers might damningly deem the "promising". I decided to include only poems that, for one reason or another, I liked. I didn't find it easy to choose.

Few poets can recall exactly the day when they began to write, but Fanthorpe could. She'd written the sort of off-the-cuff pieces that most of us have a go at, for one reason or another, if we're interested in poetry at all. Though she was always sure that she wanted to be "a writer", she'd never imagined herself as a *poet*. Poetry was a different kind of writing, and it came with the authority of a vocation, sudden and serious. 'On 18 April 1974,' she said, 'I started writing poems... I'd found the subject that

I'd been looking for all my life: the strangeness of other people, particularly neurological patients, and how it felt to be them, and to use their words.' Never having been in a neurological hospital before, her response to its strangeness was immediate. Experiences she'd never imagined suddenly surrounded her, and it was the shock of this material that 'pitchforked' her into poetry. Exasperation about the daily routines of the place and its damaged patients often generated poems, as well as pity. Anger quite often flares out in some of the early poems.

And in some of these pieces, the poet reveals herself more transparently than she does in later work; the personal reserve that developed as her work gained a public isn't yet there. Later, she seldom wrote about herself at all. It seemed to me right to allow these more personal details and attitudes to emerge; after all, she herself believed that it was the poems that mattered, not the poet; that the poems tell the truth in a way no gossip or letters or biographical narrative can. These early poems throw caution to the winds: you get a rare candour, as well as some (uncharacteristically) unsparing attitudes. There was a decidedly brisk side to this poet.

They are poems, too, that were bred in the heat of battle, during brief lunch-hours when she escaped to share with dust and spiders the hospital's redundant caravan. There was a lot of learning to do, and it wasn't all about poetry. Though she recognised the dedication and humanity of the doctors, she was instinctively on the side of the patients against the system; the daughter of a barrister, she saw herself as a witness, bound by her calling to tell the truth, about both the patients and her responses. Witnesses, by virtue of their role, often see what nobody else does, and she was always a great people-watcher. In the hospital she watched the patients; she respected their courage, their determined cheerfulness, their instinct for survival. And she listened, too: in their uncensored words she recognised the true tones of poetry. The subtle wit, the searching intellect, and the generous heart that came to characterise her later work are all here, in seed form.

E.M. Forster famously declares himself in *Two Cheers for Democracy*:

> I believe in aristocracy... if that is the right word, and if a
> democrat may use it. Not an aristocracy of power, based
> upon rank and influence, but an aristocracy of the sensitive,
> the considerate and the plucky.

These are qualities she was committed to. What she was very
much against was power. Forster noted, 'As soon as people have
power they go crooked'. Many years later, in 'Tyndale in darkness'
(*Safe as Houses*) Fanthorpe would ask 'What can you do with
power except abuse it?' And physicians, perhaps more than most,
come to assume that they have power (they have, of course: they
deal, after all, in life and death). Of certain behaviours she was
sharply critical (see, for instance, 'Management committee', or
'Diagnosis'). Despite the tone of such occasional poems, however,
she grew fond of some of the doctors. She had a ready capacity
for admiration, and because she instinctively wanted to believe
the best, wanted to take a positive line, she celebrates the good
in others, generously and even affectionately. She recognises it
wherever she finds it, and not just in people. 'A marriage', for
instance, despite its title, isn't about humans: the interdependence,
the intimacy is between 'the oldest kind of rock' and heather.
The rock is 'infinitely used / to suffering' and endures it all;
heather, the other partner, is an optimist, an opportunist, 'wiry,
irrepressible... not fussy / adapts itself to any hillside'; it is
'available to any bee', endures 'without self-consciousness the
Arctic winter'; it greets Autumn with laughter. Endurance and
survival: you make the best of your circumstances, and get on
with it as well as you can, whether you're heather or human.
Cheerfulness has her vote, and reliability – the irrepressible, the
unfussy, the adaptable.

'An honest enquiry' reveals more of the writer. Reluctant to
accept a sweeping statement at face value, she'd always challenge
it with a *But...* In 'An honest enquiry', Jesus is teaching his
disciples the worth of a human soul. Loftily, he reassures them:
'Aren't two sparrows sold for a farthing?... Don't worry... you're
of more value than many sparrows.' But Fanthorpe interrupts:

> Excuse me, I hope you don't mind,
> But how many exactly?

[...] Would you be thinking of two
Or ten? Or even twenty, maybe?

– and goes on with a rush of ornithological information (she enjoyed *knowing* things) in a maddeningly pedantic way. And she makes it clear that she admires sparrows, which of course is totally off the point of the gospel story:

I like them. Reliable types,

Always there, not like the moody migrants,
And always cheerful, or give that impression [...]

'Venus' birds, you know,' she says, then adds apologetically, 'though perhaps / You don't want to know about that – 'And after all this comical know-it-all stuff she ends with disarming humility

What makes you think
I could be worth even one of them?

Suddenly the poem turns from the comic to the deeply serious. This last-minute inversion of the mood of the poem was a characteristic Fanthorpe movement. 'Patience Strong' (*Side Effects*) ends in a similar way. Robin Lane Fox, reviewing *Voices Off* in the *Financial Times* in 1984, asks 'Who will [...] move you, going straight for the emotions? Unhesitatingly I name U.A. Fanthorpe as the poet who can suddenly hit you below the heart.'

God gets the sharp end of the poet's tongue in 'Complaints Department'. A sort of poetic doodle to pass the time, this was written when she was a temp at Hoover's complaints department, before she began work at the hospital and before poetry properly took over. Having quite entertainingly described the plight of an unhappy client, she ends

God, can't you do something
For this harassed client of yours? [...]
                    I
Can send her an engineer.
What can you do?

Perhaps the nearest thing to a frankly confessional poem in this selection is 'Apology for clarity'. An unpretentious little poem, it acknowledges her sense of her own deficiencies, her artlessness and lack of personal subtlety. True, she was herself no good at all at dissimulation. She presents her own inadequacies as if she were a house:

> One look inside
>
> Shows curtains, walls,
> Fixtures and fittings too.
> I am the sort of house
> You look straight through [...]
>
> I'm unambiguous,
> I've no defence.

And again the end turns the tale inside out. It's about vulnerability, but there's no pathos behind the final half-dozen monosyllables:

> All other homes
> Can hide behind opaque
> Expensive glass. Mine is
> The sort to break.

You can also see her love of words – ordinary words. She preferred the short word to the long, the simple word to the complex, the downright Anglo-Saxon to the polysyllabic Latinate. Though the perspective of the poem is very different, 'Cured depressive' is similarly 'fragile'; in his tidy suit, the patient himself is a present for the doctor, in wrapping paper. But both appearance and wrapping are delicate as glass; any minute now he may shatter.

This nimble ability to turn the tables is a useful gift for any poet. Unpoetic audiences, seduced by the comedy, would be hit 'below the heart' by the sudden transition to the serious. She'd learnt this long ago from Shakespeare. 'A confused noise within' is a very early "found" poem – a dramatic uncensored extract from the rambling confabulation of patients. The final words are hers, and painfully raw:

> O let me not be afraid
> May I not run out of patience
> > Of love
> > Of fortitude
> I too ate ere.

'Crab', another candid poem, admits that she studies 'the art /
Of adjusting to what others / might expect'. And no, it's not
about social manipulation – far from it. She simply didn't miss
a thing. One of the reasons why she was good at 'adjusting' was
that there was always something of the frustrated dramatist in
Fanthorpe. She always hoped to write a real play – not just the
sort of light-hearted things she wrote for school productions,
such as the comedy *Inside Story* (played by members of staff, and
indeed revived more than once after we'd left Cheltenham), or
Stratfantasia, her celebration of Shakespeare's quater-centenary
in 1964. Poetry opened for her a kind of dramatic possibility
that she hadn't expected, prompted, she admitted, by Browning.

In form, the earliest poems are brief rhymed bulletins from
her strange new situation, many of them about her bizarre
companions. Most often they are four-liners, and like ballads,
neatly organised and shaped, the sort of music we're all familiar
with from nursery-rhyme days. Often at this early stage her
response is one of dismay at the parts played by doctors,
patients, ambulance men, social workers, nurses; even by the
matron's cats. In writing these cameos of hospital life, she took
the nearest form to hand. There wasn't much time, in her forty-
minute lunch-hour, to experiment with form – and a ballad
would serve to get down quickly the things she needed to say.
Such simple forms were off-the-peg clothes that would fit on to
almost any topic, without undue subtlety. Metrical experiment
and fine tuning took longer, came later, as she learnt how to
tailor her days more usefully: 'Phoenix' analyses what she began
to understand she was doing:

> Around my day work slides its eggshell shape,
> Whose spurious logic seems exact as rhyme.
> The morning's post is waiting; no escape
> From work's irrelevance till coffee-time.
> New outpatients; the anxious telephone;
> Lists, letters, EEG reports to type.
> At one I have an hour when I'm my own,
> Then reassume my clerkly stereotype.
> This punctuated life fits oddly well.
> The things that really count are kept in play;
> I lurk contented in my fragile shell,

Knowing that I can break it any day.
Freedom unnerves; servitude sets me free
To hatch the phoenix that I want to be.

The four-liner could also be, subtly, poetically useful: in 'Diagnosis' the dismissive tone of the poem mirrors the dismissive tone of the doctor; it serves to distance the reader, and to objectify the patient. In 'For Sappho' the form offers enough freedom and space to race through centuries of history, just as the sustained preoccupation with fire is right for both Sappho and her inextinguishable power.

'T-group' she wrote in pre-poetic days, in 1970: like 'Complaints Department', it's a quick sketch to entertain herself. It uses that other reliable music, the iambic pentameter. Some of the early hospital poems also find this an accommodating shape, handy for more complex thought, as, for instance, in 'Defeated'. For description – the meditative and leisurely 'Durdham Down' or the reflective intricacies of 'Writer's garden' – iambic pentameter offered space and a more laconic movement. Rhyme, helpful for the earliest acerbic arrows, is gradually beginning to be replaced by something more flexible. The shock of the new was giving way to a more thoughtful, less epigrammatic style, and Fanthorpe was beginning to deal with a wider range of subjects. 'Gay Christians' is relaxed, discursive; and in the confiding personal moments (in 'Eavesdropper') and the musical, leisurely meditation on George Herbert's church at Bemerton you can see narrative and soliloquy all escaping from their hurried tight patterns. 'Infidelity' offers a sort of half-way house, its rough uneven pentameters carrying the tale forward effectively, movingly. She very quickly frees herself from the early rhymes and rhythms; reading these poems you can almost feel her throwing off the once supporting scaffoldings that began to limit what she wanted to say.

Or what the poem wants to say. She trusts the poems themselves to dictate both what they want to say, and how to say it. All the shackles have fallen off in 'The head housemaid tells the receptionist a joke'. The targets – the 'enemies' – tend to be found in the patterned poems now: 'Headmistress' is relaxed enough in its in rough pentameters, but it has a savage metrically exact conclusion. Rhyme begins to be reserved, too, for comedy, for 'To the Holy Ghost'. 'Fairy-tale' is once-upon-a-time-subverted, free of any form; and parody's useful for the sustained voice of the bureaucrat in 'O and M study: the boatman'.

Two-liners, three-liners were patterns she used quite early: the final line could carry a lot of quiet weight. In 'The golden girls', with its short last lines, you get a sense of increasing trap as these lines grow briefer with each verse. 'On behalf of Chaos' uses a variation; the long last lines here mirror the subject. And contempt creeps into the terse last lines of 'Administrator' and 'Song of the flea'.

Quickly she discovered that she could play a lot of different tunes on a lot of different instruments – as she says in the conversational 'Job description: poet'

> You are surrounded
> By the subject, life. The tools of this trade
>
> Are common property: five senses,
> One brain, one heart, and words,
> Words, words.

The voices developed; the organisation, the diction became increasingly sure-footed. The subject-matter seemed to be endless: everything had its voice, from God and the Holy Ghost to the Head Housemaid, from George Herbert to a flea. She writes about the feckless and the frail, the arrogant and the obsessive; about courage and danger and pomposity and gentleness. And about herself, and her own sense of self-discovery. She found the hospital horrifying, and funny, and tender and absurd. When things got her down she wrote poems to cheer herself up – notably 'Not my best side' (in *Side Effects*), and 'Only here for the bier' (in *Standing To*).

With a lifetime of poetry reading behind her, a lifetime's love of words and history, and a rapidly increasing command of the mechanics of the job (both jobs, poet and receptionist) at last she'd discovered who she was. 'In these circumstances,' she said, 'poetry happened to me [...] The long boredom of slowly discovering who I was and what I could do was over: poetry struck during my first month behind the desk.'

Her targets, then as later, are the self-satisfied, the pompous; her concerns the concerns of the unnoticed, the (sometimes literally, as in 'Linguist') voiceless. But her sympathies are wide. Though consultants often come off worst, there is genuine admiration and insight in 'Consultant's holiday'. It's a transitional poem, moving away from rhyme and yet using it almost clandestinely. She sees the consultant as a soldier, sounding the war notes that came so often later. The consultant has his enemies, weapons, allies; his holidays are spent on a 'different front', in Scotland, amid 'distance, loneliness and cold'. Though the war – or war vocabulary – crept into the corners, it wasn't often a subject at this time. The big important subjects came later. For her, then, it was the everyday mosaic of small concerns, small betrayals – for instance, how she found that much of madness suggested sanity; the corners, sad and solitary, of others' lives, the insignificant "ordinary" lives that we all have and seldom notice. The fragility of the patients, of course, is always a matter of concern.

Voices of all sorts of people echo in the poems: not only patients and doctors, but literary figures, the long-dead and the immediate present – and of course her own, often funny. This isn't a poet taking herself seriously (as poets sometimes do); it's a poet enjoying writing, about anything and everything that comes to hand. She was shy, but people interested her, and the hospital provided everything, from cleaners and seriously disturbed patients to the magical realms of the medical hierarchy, from the god-like and eminent to the convoluted lives of the lesser professionals. She had an eye for the absurd, an ear for the human voice, a taste for irony and a love of comedy – and a tender heart for the human misery that washed around her all the time. Like the 'Dead social worker' she knew – and needed to know – two languages.

And of course in the 70s there was feminism. 'Defeated' her first feminist poem, is a rambling, passionate poem about the oppressed race of women, taught by their masters to distrust each other, deprived by their masters of their language ('all our words are theirs'). But – 'strangely', she observes, their masters 'watch us always'; they 'fear us still'. In the early 70s this wasn't just a rant; it seemed uncomfortably accurate. 'Fairy-tale' gives

15

feminist concerns another kind of liberation – the comic; along with 'Woman's world', 'The brides of Christ', 'Sir' – and the jokey 'To the Holy Ghost'. No territory is sacred, from the gruesomeness of the leuco-coagulation 'Demonstration' to what the 'Management Committee' ate for lunch.

But she is invariably just: we also gain some sense of the tedious hidden toil of the consultants, in 'Eavesdropper'. She is observant, but not partisan. We see the apprehensive patients, discussing the 'Problem picture', in the waiting-room – but we also learn what the in-patients get up to (especially at weekends), for the patients, a varied lot, are very much like the rest of us: the desperate little Welshwoman, endlessly 'stroking her wrists', the killer, looming harmlessly in his socks, the sexual delinquent who sounds so exciting but turns out to be merely a pathetic little pilferer, 'in charge of a capable spinster'. The inherent contradictions in the Hippocratic oath lurk horribly in the violence meted out to 'Miss Morris'.

Her own uncensored feelings are fiercely alive in 'Typist' and 'The receptionist'; 'Gingerbread' celebrates her joy at escaping from teaching; the sociological subtleties of the role of the temp (which she was before she began work at the hospital) are neatly analysed in 'Poem for temps'. And one of the wittiest pieces is her bureaucratic take on Charon's job, in 'O and M study: the boatman'.

She deals with more difficult subjects, such as the uncomfortable reality of betrayal, (in 'Infidelity'); she's very conscious of the essential fear and loneliness of gay men, in the early hostile world of the 70s, as they wistfully ponder the mystery of marriage vows – 'it must be great to be so sure'. The irony of the situation of the successful novelist, in 'Writer's garden' – whose apparently comfortable surroundings depend on the frailty of imagination – isn't lost on her. And the idealised setting of that writer's garden was certainly not for her; 'The bowl of roses' sprang from my naivety. As excited by the outpouring of the poems as she was, I'd presumed (in my conventional way) that a poet would like to work in the peacefulness of a study, with roses on the desk, a view of the garden, etc, etc. Not a bit of it. In the midst of life was where Fanthorpe wanted to be, surrounded by all the paraphernalia, all the inconsistencies and absurdities of the everyday world. There was to be no nun-like seclusion for her – unless you count the forty minutes' lunch-hour in the decrepit caravan.

These are all apprentice pieces; she'd be the first to dismiss them. But they are nevertheless remarkable for their qualities of close observation, imaginative sympathy, and the lightness of their touch, both narrative and descriptive – all the qualities "real"' poets need. Above all there's an engaging infectious excitement and energy that attracts the reader, whatever their subject or tone or form – a sense of life, of experiment, the joyous exploration of a new-found skill and a new landscape, a new range of characters and unexpected situations.

Subjects more demanding and difficult came later, and with them greater technical skill. But the hospital gave her poems their their first breath, and even in this improbable cradle their features are recognisably Fanthorpe.

R.V. BAILEY

A confused noise within

ANNE   I ATE ERE

ANDY   'Scuse me, it's me again. Is today Tuesday or Wednesday? Tuesday the 14th.

JANE   *(Enters office silently. Stands very close. Nods her head)*

JOE   This place is like a bloody concentration camp. If I had the use of my legs I'd get out of this bloody dump to Bath, where I am respected.

ANNE   WHY AM I ERE

ANDY   'Scuse me, it's me again. Tuesday the 14th you said? So tomorrow is the 15th? Jill's coming t'day

JANE   *(As before)*

JOE   It's that sister with the glasses. Who does she think she is? Bloody woman. Pissing bloody woman. What I want to do today is to draw me invalid allowance, me pension.

ANNE   I DON'T KNOW WHY I'M ERE

ANDY   'Scuse me, it's me again. Jill's coming today, Look, on Tuesday it says *Jill coming later*. On Wednesday it says *Jill not coming*.

JANE   *(As before)*

JOE   How old do you think I am? I'm 39. I was born on February the 28th, 1942. I was in the Welsh Guards. I was. If I had the use of my legs, I'd bloody show 'em.

ANNE   I'VE AD ENOUGH.

ANDY   'Scuse me, it's me again. On Wednesday it says *Jill not coming*. Thank you very much. Jill's coming later. I'll remember that, is it Tuesday today or Wednesday?

JANE   *(As before)*

JOE   I'm a Catholic I am. When you get married in a Catholic
        church you marry till death you do part. My ex-wife's a
        funny woman. I found her in bed with another woman.

> O let me not be afraid.
> May I not run out of patience
>   Of love
>   Of fortitude
> I too ate ere.

A funny set-up

Elderly chap in a cap
Removed only (under protest)
For an EEG, crammed back on
Instantly, afterwards,
Being a piece of him.

Underlip protrudes in scorn.
Unmoved by rank, or the flighty
Niceties of medical etiquette.
Consultants become *that woman*.
Reverence is reserved for *Sunday*;
Not for the nurses' sanctum.

We dare not question
What failing brings him here,
Though even lay eyes spot
His limp, his gloved left hand,
His puff belly, his pop eyes.
Armed in his own assessments,
He has dismissed ours:
A funny set-up, this.

A nurse coaxes him
With pills. He consumes them slowly,
Censoriously. Lamely
We go our ways.
We have been weighed
In his cracked balance, and found wanting
What he has got.

A high wind

There was a high wind at my birth,
All the signposts slewed sideways
On their hinges.

In the blizzard of infancy
I looked for love and found it
In hard covers.

In the adolescent whirlwind
I looked for learning. It was
In other schools.

Universities cowered in
My stormy youth. Learning was
Terribly old.

A marriage

One of them is the oldest kind of rock,
Archaic, remote, and infinitely used
To suffering. All that happened later –
Animals, plants, fish, the crawling worm,
Coal, limestone, insects, and the dinosaur
Sea-urchins, sponges, mammoths, ammonites,
Evergreen plants, and man – occurred
After she came. Her pre-Cambrian profile
Has watched, and not been comforted
By anything. She knows it all
Means suffering. But hers goes further back
And when you're more than four
Hundred million years old, it's hard to see
(What most you want) an end to your existence.
Enduring godforsaken,
Her image is the far northeast of Scotland
Where nothing grows.

The other is the heather
Wiry, irrepressible. Discouraged
By fire from flourishing in one place
It adjourns to another. Heather's not fussy,
Adapts itself to any hillside;
Available to any bee, endures
Without self-consciousness the Arctic winter,
Salutes Autumn with a volley
Of pink and raucous laughter.

Administrator

Underling too long, though finally you made it
To top dog, you knew the system too well
To bark authentically.

You, the expert on short cuts, on first-name terms
With the influential – stores, post-room, porters; you
Who knew how to fix it,

Whose good deeds were always shady, like
The fiddled day off for Christmas shopping, which
Was rightfully ours;

You who scrounged, never spent, who shook
With fright before committees, who always forgot
Your own authority;

Who dared not sanction our electric kettles,
Whose kindnesses were home-made, compensation
For your servile failure
To improve anything.

All Souls

The dead live in the back parts of our cortex.
When we provoke them they come out
Hallooing *We thought you'd forgotten us –*
Gosh, isn't this fun!

We provoke them. We go where we last went
With them. And the harmless, innocent places
Are habitats of ghosts. And the ghosts come gallumphing,
Isn't this fun?

And it is fun, for them. The bridges, theatres,
The shop where they bought that raincoat, all surviving,
All happy to be there still. And the ghosts whooping,
We thought you'd forgotten us...

It is we, the living, who daub over all
The glaze of guilt. We went on being alive.
We have forgotten the fun, forgotten that raincoat. But no:
We haven't forgotten.

An honest enquiry

Jesus said to his disciples: *'Are not two sparrows sold for a farthing? And one of them shall not fall on the ground without your father... Fear ye not, therefore, ye are of more value than many sparrows.'*

Excuse me, I hope you don't mind,
But how many exactly?

I mean, many is not exactly
A precise word, is it?

So would you be thinking of two
Or ten? Or even twenty, maybe?

Because when you think of the number
Of clutches in a year

(Three, say, and say five at a time)
That adds up to quite a lot,

You must admit. On the other hand,
I like them. Reliable types,

Always there, not like the moody migrants,
And always cheerful, or give that impression,

Fossicking around in dust, drinking,
Tearing bits of moss off roofs,

Venus' birds, you know, though perhaps
You don't want to know about that –

Anyway, friendly citizens. What makes you think
I could be worth even one of them?

Apology for clarity

I am too clear.
I don't know how to hide
My meaning from your view.
One look inside

Shows curtains, walls,
Fixtures and fittings too.
I am the sort of house
You look straight through

And see the lawn,
The flowers and boundary fence.
I'm unambiguous,
I've no defence.

All other homes
Can hide behind opaque
Expensive glass. Mine is
The sort to break.

At Cadbury

The knights keep the mound.
The native cattle, with their slow
Honourable look. Saracen swallows,
Bending argent and gules as they swoop,
Their winged scimitars slashing
The impassive air.

A young rabbit, too,
By the blackberries with the same
White badge, clearly comic page to somebody;
Him I nearly caught. But the bird,
Unidentified, hawkish, that flew off, was master
Of the incident.

Where men didn't come.
Tennyson over Severn in laurelled Caerleon,
Sir Thomas in Newgate (whom God
Send good deliverance), and later White,
Dulling Irish exile with a red setter
And the DNB.

No need to come here.
Camelot towers' pennons wave anywhere.
This is simple Cadbury, on whose banks,
Nettled, cow-patted, introspection
Is impossible. You have to look out, to
The Apple Island,

Whose weird finger draws
Over twelve miles of commonplace Somerset
Magic conclusions. Arthur, perhaps,
Or somebody, looked out too,
At the grave of his long bones,
Which were not buried,

Though resurrected.
To come is to believe too much,
Or nothing. For here the unassertive landscape,
The web of sky, invisible fixed stars,
Braced in significance, discharge on us
Their need to doubt.

Boarding kennels

Here we lodge love when it grows inconvenient.
Here behind bars it will wait for us while we
Go away for the weekend
Or run up to London
For a round of theatres,
Or fly off on our summer holidays,
Or pursue any other occupation
Where love gets in the way.

Love will wait till we come back
(Being behind bars it hasn't much choice).
It will be fed, exercised, kept
Warm, preserved from all the dangers
Incident upon loving and being
Free. In fact, when we see it again, love
Will have put on weight. When it sees us
Love will leap in such an agony
Of joy as to spoil completely, in retrospect,
All the pleasure that we had on holiday
Without it.

Complaints Department

Is that Complaints, please? Miss,
I'm having trouble over my
Washing-machine. It rattles
When I turn it on, then it shakes,
And leaks over the kitchen floor.
It started like this last Tuesday,
And your engineer came, spent an hour
Here, and he said it'd
Be all right after. But it's not all right.
How it is, Miss, my dad's
Incontinent, and I have to keep
His sheets washed for him. Also
My husband's a bit fussy – you know, dear,
How they are – and the kids, they're
Always under my feet. I get
Worried about things.

Will I be in
When your engineer calls? Oh yes, dear,
I'm always in.

          Is that Complaints, please?
God, can't you do something
For this harassed client of yours
With her old dad who shakes,
And her husband who rattles, and
The kids, who probably leak over the floor?
Now even her washing-machine
Is letting her down. I
Can send her an engineer.
What can you do?

Consultant's holiday

His enemies: death, suicide, the slow
Phlegmatic nonexistence of despair,
Obsession's endless wood of private fears.

His soldiers: bored, promiscuous, with low
Morale and bad feet, not the type to share
Heroic vigils on the mind's frontiers.

His weapons: therapy of various sorts,
Drugs, treatment, hobbies. Such arms
Sometimes explode, and injure his own men.

His allies: friendly tribes, whose dullness thwarts
Elaborate manoeuvres with alarms
Of missing cats, or time for tea again.

His leave's spent fighting on a different front,
Tracking down distance, loneliness and cold
In their Scots fastness. These he traps and kills,

But when time's up, returns to his own hunt,
To find his side demoralised and old,
Despair and death glowing like daffodils.

Crab

Born under the Crab,
I am drawn to inland waters.

I like the damp ambiguous
Reaches of Sedgemoor, Romney's locked
And misty churches, the strict Fenland dykes
That drown men.

I have never known
If my house is on rock or sand.

I have never known my sex or
My true name. I study the art
Of adjusting myself to what others
Might expect.

The zodiac is
To blame for my sidelong glances.

How can I, who am nothing and
Nowhere, love your bold design? Marsh,
Lake and quiet waterway surrender;
Land claims me.

Cured depressive

Here's a present for the doctor
Wrapped in a smart summer suit,
Matching socks and tie and hanky,
Polish lavished on each boot

Labelled *Merry Christmas*, doctor,
I'm the present you deserve
I'm the healed and happy patient
Fit and free in every nerve.

See him in his wrapping paper
Hair cut carefully as grass
Read the maker's label, doctor:
Careful. Fragile. This is glass.

Defeated

(also called 'Lost Tribe')

In war defeated by a brilliant race
So many years ago, my tribe is dumb.
We have no memories of another life.
Our gods are lost. Our conquerors gave us theirs
And so we love it. But their god hates us.

Our race is silent. Poets and musicians
Our rulers are, painters and master-builders.
They heal, they teach, thrust mines into the earth,
Harness the seasons in their fertile fields.
They govern. They are masters of our world.

The land, the laws, are theirs. We have no names
To hand on to our children. In the past
Some few rebelled, but rebels never thrive.
Suppressing them is easy. Old ones burn,
Young ones are choked to death with pregnancies

Our language faded from us long ago
And all our words are theirs. We mispronounce,
In all these centuries have never learned
Their way of thinking. Though we love their art,
Revere their science and their hardihood,
We dare not rival them in anything.

We have no past. Theirs has been handed down,
Its honour and disgrace, to learned ones
As lessons for the future. Ours is secret.
No one dare write it, for it would be treason,
And so it's lost. Our faint revolts find space
In records of our conquerors, but not
Our unrebellious silent centuries.

Strangely, they fear us still. We have no weapons
And yet they watch us always. Most of us
Have a perpetual guard, who stays by us
And shares our living quarters. When we talk
With others of our tribe, they feel afraid,
But never tell us what it is they fear.

They tell us that without them we should die
And we believe them. We distrust each other
At their instruction. How can we imagine
Our tribe united, independent, free
To be itself, when our fierce masters have
Defeated our imagination? All
That we can do is die, and this we do
Symbolically. We wish each child we bear
May never share in our captivity.
And so we want no daughters. Only sons.

Demonstration of leuco-coagulation treatment
to a conference of the Royal Society of Psychiatrists

He lies steady as a marble man
In a cold aisle. At his crusader's feet
Obsession dozes. Camouflaged and neat,
Stained by a life's campaigns to muted tan,
He rules his sad-boned face as best he can,
Knowing the trippers, showily discreet,
Have read the Baedeker of his defeat.
The courier to this gay caravan
Explains the contours of his fractured mind.
The conduit for his shame and her concern
Runs through her finger on his pumping wrist.
Properly scientific, they're resigned
To public viewing. Bright above them burn
The lunch-flushed faces of psychiatrists.

[This event took place on 17 April 1975. RVB]

Diagnosis

This was a fairly attractive although vacant-faced and
sycophantically smiling female with mild scoliosis and a
rolling gait around the right hip.

Well, Angela, so now you know
What the nice doctor thought of you.
A female. Yes, he knew your sex;
He saw that you were smiling, too.

Fairly attractive. Who's the judge?
And who's he judging? What did you
Think of this solemn mature male?
Or did he simper back at you?

Poor Angela. Your vacant face
Seems sad to me. Where could you find
Beauty and learning to impress
His highly-educated mind?

Caravan-born, council-house bred,
Hardened to ignorance and want,
It's to your credit, Angela,
That you turned out a sycophant.

Durdham Down

Lorries flow murmurous around its fringe.
At half-past one the football pitch is bare.
Mud's overtaking grass. The flat green stems
Are bent back on themselves. Earth pushes through.
The trees grow steadily at their own pace;
The water tower, braced at its proper height,
Observes their progress from its bastion
Where Bristol laps and moans up Blackboy Hill.

We walk towards it. No one else about.
The city keeps its distance. The young dog,
Her breath before her like an extra nose,
Quarters the ground. Free from the drag of smell,
She courses, heavy head slightly askew
And long jaw vacant. Aiming straight at me
Her vague brown half-a-mile-off distant shape
Becomes familiar Shandy as I blink.

A flight of starlings feeding in the grass
Blows off at her approach, hangs in the air
With sunlight flashing on each well-drilled wing,
Then slots into another feeding place
Like automatic birds. Gravely I weave
A magic circle on the open down,
As if my footsteps held the city back.

Eavesdropper

He is his own most
Permanent patient. The rest
Get discharged in the end, or
Die, or don't bother to come back.
But still, beyond these
Changes, the perpetual blurred
Dialogues behind his door
Between two voices: the patient,
Reedy, confiding, often stopping
To think; and the repeating voice,
Masterful, mechanical, loud,
Of the doctor. When I intrude
On the consultation, no one
Is speaking at all, but a tired
Elderly man passively sips
A cup of tea, while the tape
Waits for one of his selves.

Fairy-tale

Suddenly there was a tremendous
Wallop from the enchanted hedge,
And in strolled the Princess
With her axe. She marched over
To the Prince, and kissed him
Full on his beautiful mouth.

The Prince woke up, of course.
So did everyone else.
They all complained in chorus:

We can't have this, it's quite
Against the rules. This hussy had acted
In a masculine, independent way.
We can't have our Prince brought
Back into circulation by a mere
Female.

The Princess was quite
Casual about it. *OK*, she said,
Be like that, then. And went off
To rescue someone less choosy.

The Prince and his court gave
A sigh of relief, and went
Back to their beauty sleep.

For Sappho

Your mouth spoke fire. Aegean seas
Weren't deep enough to put you out.
You shone like suns. The Isles of Greece
Basked in your fierce poetic drought.

Death banked you down; but you had left
Bonfires behind you. And they flamed
Across the hilltops of the world,
Signalling poetry untamed.

Cool clerics thought your fires unfit,
And quenched them with a holy chill;
Some few ambiguous escaped,
And blithely burned their readers still.

Late scholars grovelling in ash
At Oxyrhynchus found a few
Cindery fragments. By their heat
They knew that these were sparks of you.

Words that had scorched were scorched themselves,
Torn into strips for rubbish piles,
Or wadded in the carcasses
Of stuffed Egyptian crocodiles.

What conflagration flamed in you
That such a fieriness still lingers?
We breathe upon these scraps of ash
And find that they have burned our fingers.

From a bestiary

Take care. I am a lion
Clawed and tongued gules.
I am fierce,

Rampant, regardant. I roar
In the hushed forests of the night
And scare squirrels.

I shall rip you, regally,
In pieces, whenever you
Make a mistake

With my appointment book.
I don't trust you an inch
You must date

And time every telephone
Message, or I shall butcher you
Bloodily.

My roll-top desk is locked
Against intruders. I answer
No phone calls ever

Bloody woman, I roar,
To the hushed forests of the night,
No she can't see me.

If I do relent,
Purr leoninely, consoling her
As only lion-hearts can

You must pretend not to notice.
Touching inconsistency is
Part of my nature.

Sometimes my lair is in
Matron's office. I lurk there
Barricaded behind nurses
And cups of tea.

Gay Christians

Upper room religion. One disciple
Comes hot from his shift, smelling
Of cooking fat. The sick man
Is restless behind the partition.
They hear him sneezing.

In his experienced voice the leader
Chats about dates. They expand
Into another identity. Appearance here
Equals confession. Strangers know
What friends must never.

A scratch lot, whose liaisons
Are casual as cats', they ponder
The mystery of marriage-vows.
It must be great to be so sure.
Disciples whom Jesus loves.

They tell mild misogynist jokes,
Muse on cottaging's dangers, genuflect
In the direction of St Oscar. Now street lamps
Lighten the darkness; Bill is scared
To be out at night.

Someone will take him home.
Let us pray. Holy and hopeless, they stand,
Whom neither man nor God will leave alone,
Praying for love, joy, peace,
And for their enemies.

George Herbert's church at Bemerton

Ages, ages ago
when I hankered after obedience, virtue,
moderation, goodwill,
a pilgrimage of a sort to the parish
of somebody quiet.

Out there, crisp April fields
and the grandly distant spire not beckoning
but absolute. In here,
pitch-pine; prayers sandwiched in weary covers; dust.

But still this thing shuffles
in wayward mind: a tortoiseshell butterfly
adding its widow's mite
to the shabby colours the sun was brushing
on to a gothick sill.

With bent legs eyelash-thin
having bivouacked in musty crevices
the whole of winter's length
to march out single, domino borders frayed,
against a fortress gules!

Whether to let it dull
its sapphires on red glass, and die believing
salvation lay beyond
or catch it up and cast it free to perish
on the true sun's white barb?

Sweet temperate Herbert, what epitome
might you have found in this?
I closed your door not yours.
Creation will not tutor us as it used.
Ruled by its cold *I am*
We've lost your grasp of heaven.

Gingerbread maker

There is nothing to take the gilt off the gingerbread
Like setting up in trade as a gingerbread maker.
My gingerbread is English Lit. I loved it devotedly
Until I forced it to keep me in coals, milk and bread.
Then it grew a trifle stale. It wilted, and sprouted mildew.
Poor thing! It had enough reason. There was I
Droning on about patterns of imagery, and scansion,
Worrying about pupils' behaviour in theatre foyers,
Preserving postcards of Dove Cottage, listening
To the late-night television programmes, making
Other people do the same, and cracking
Dry little occupational jokes of quotations.

Now I've cut loose, the gingerbread is golden
All over again; I can gorge on it, and never worry
About its moral tone.

Headmistress

Ten years of too much power have fattened her.
She's twice the woman who came, new and shy
And ignorant, hoping to help us all.
Since then she's built, and failed with girls, and built
Some more. Bricks have a more effective span.
Detractors will remember tempers lost,
Children misunderstood, teachers offended.
But bricks, less sensitive, only recite
Biographies of those who put them there,
And so her kingdom grows. No need to ask
Where's the naive enthusiast who came
To do her job? She ate her long ago,
Now builds her brick memorial to provide
Accommodation for a powerful corpse.

House-hunting

Some are the pampered mistresses of kings.
Cedars conceal their private parts, and deer
Walk softly down their corridors of power.

Some are stockbrokers' sweethearts, trimly thatched,
Smelling of mignonette and rich cigars.
Jaguars lie in wait outside their doors.

Some are the graduated wives of young
Promising men. Their flawless Georgian paint
Gleams fiercely from their neurasthenic walls.

All are too dear for me. But something lurks
Around the margins of the possible,
Unloved, with shaggy gutters, and a stray

Improper charm, unfit for stockbrokers,
Or kings, or men of promise. Something waits
Hidden behind her hedge, for someone's kiss.

In-patients

Like children, when it's sunny they behave,
Play ball games on the grass, run the canteen
Without much obvious embezzlement,
Are regular with drugs, use no obscene
Words to alarm the matron, kick the cat
Only in private, go for jolly walks
In healthy groups, return in time for tea,
Cooperate in therapeutic talks.

Like children, when it's rainy they are bad,
Forgetful of the needs of indoor plants,
Ignore their visitors, smoke endlessly,
Confine their repartee to *won't* and *shan't*,
Form tearstained queues outside the nurses room,
Drink gin at night, and set fire to their sheets,
Abscond, break windows, commit suicide,
Involve us in their infantile defeats.

Like parents, we don't take them seriously.
We shrug their tantrums off as children's play,
We speak to them in kindergarten tones,
Deaf to the insult under all we say.
And when they mimic adult games, and kiss
And talk of marriage, we applaud *How nice!*
Joyfully yoking two unstable minds,
Our wedding gift a birth-control device.

Like anchorites, they guard their silent cells,
Devoted to the rituals of despair.
The blood-soaked stone walls are inviolable,
And laymen cannot penetrate to share
The vigils these abandoned saints must bear,
Who straddle the irreconcilable
Vaults of mankind in our hygienic air,
And gasp their litanies to our dry bells.

Infidelity

Our father loved small boats. His ten-foot dinghy
Was clinker-built, had ocean-going oars
And a rare Swedish outboard. Every winter,
Well-greased palms tended her. And every summer
She took our father up to Teddington
And back again. A distance of a mile.

Our father was a heavy man, a judge,
A barrister, a man of substance. When
He boarded her, the dinghy nearly foundered.
We blushed for him, and scrambled to the bows
But childish bones couldn't redress his weight.

My father loved the manners of the river,
Port-to-port, he'd teach us, and *give way*.
This sweet correctness never won him credit
With Tiddler the fat waterman, who ruled
The mooring raft. All day he brooded there,
Brown, shirtless, his stomach sticking far
Out in contempt, rescuing novices
With casual boathook. Rescuing father, too,
When up at Teddington his Swede once more
Betrayed him. Flicking through the waves
Tiddler would come, scorn apparent in
The angle of his stomach. And with one
Negligent pull of greasy twine, he'd rouse
The faithless Swede, then skim back to his raft,
Leaving our father to toil slowly back,
Publicly shamed. Or so we felt. Our father
Wooed Tiddler ceaselessly with cigarettes
And tactful tips, but never won his heart.

We, like the Swede, were Tiddler's and not his.
Children and outboards reverence the strong,
Despise the meek. Dear father, only now

I understand how strong you were, to bow
So humbly to the elementary skill
Tiddler possessed. And he perhaps was dumb
To say how proud he was of knowing you.
Did he perform so well to justify
Your praise? I'll never know. The boat is sold
And you are dead, and Tiddler, if he lives,
Must need his shirt by now. All I have left
Is the sad taste of treason in my mouth,
And a dislike of boathooks.

Introducing...

This little man
Five foot one in his socks
Is: a killer.

These burly chaps
Eyeing the little man:
Are warders.

This starchy girl,
Professional with pill
And medicine glass,

Watching the man
As painfully he drinks,
Swallows and drinks

And gets it down,
The necessary pill,
Is: a Sister.

The pill he takes,
The big pink pill, is: for
Travel sickness.

The travel he
Needs it for: his journey
Back to prison.

The distance he
Will cover on the way
Is: three whole miles.

The pill he takes
So seriously is:
A placebo.

And we who watch
Straightforward and intent are:
Part of the joke.

Job description: poet

A cheap art. All you need is something
To write on, and with. In my case
Yesterday's clinic list, a hospital biro.

You don't need a north light, clay,
Scored paper, silence, sympathy.
You can do it wherever you are. You don't need

Freedom, or friends, or fellow artists
To perform what you create. You are surrounded
By the subject, life. The tools of this trade

Are common property: five senses,
One brain, one heart, and words,
Words, words. That there are problems

I don't deny: inner solitude,
Emptiness, despair. But remember, poetry is a cheap art.
You can't expect to get anything for nothing.

Linguist

The smashed voice roars inside the ruined throat
Behind the mangled face. Voice of the wild,
Voice of the warthog calling to his mates,

Wordless, huge-volumed, sad. We can't make out
A meaning (though his wife can). Solitary
He sits, shrouded in his vast noise. How strange

To make so much, none of it any use
To fragile human ears, except to mis-
Inform. For we all make the obvious

And wrong deduction: *this poor chap is mad.*
He doesn't talk like us. He can't be sane.
And yet he is. Look in his serious eyes;

He understands. Reads magazines. He bawls
Obliterated meanings at his wife.
O yes, she says, *a sundial would be nice.*

That's what he'd like. A silent clock that speaks
The solemn language of the sun to grass
And garden-lovers with a turn for sums.

Management committee

Drink lures them:
Dry sherry, Burgundy,
Port and black coffee.

With a flap
Of their well-filled black sleeves
They arrive, snuffing

Prawn cocktails,
Fillet steak garni, and
Meringue chantilly.

Gorged eyes peer
Gummily at fellow
Consultants only,

Are too dim
To grasp the faint outlines
Of inferiors.

Expensive
Shoes make the stairs tremble.
No sound can compete

With the dull
Assertive roar of their
Burgundy voices.

Now they've gone.
Their spoor: a cigar butt
In a slopped saucer.
Meeting at night

We meet

By a pillarbox no longer there
Under a moon that stopped eight years ago.

The road,
I suppose, is still the same,
The pavement, the weeds, and the night-quiet gardens.

The barn
On the other side has gone.
To replace it, the tranquil bitch, snuffing dry leaves.

I'm here
And there, the same name,
The same hands and feet – you'd know me still.

I wish
I could help, tell you
It'll be all right, you'll survive it to become me.

But you
Are pinned there, in the past,
And never knew you'd walk into my future.

Miss Morris

At seventy Miss Morris came to Death,
Who took her gently, as her time was up.
Her senile heart dealt with its final breath,
And then retired. But this old-fashioned cup
Was not allowed. Resourceful doctors tore
The dignity of dying from the dead;
Sinewy nurses flung her to the floor
And gave her cardiac massage. *Look*, they said,
There's something there. Defibrillation shocked
Her body, and she lived. She died again.
And lived. And died. And lived. Until she clocked
Her thirteenth resurrection, and in pain
Achieved extinction. Her life-saving bruises
Testify man can't die, until Man chooses.

Misunderstood

I devoted a long and arduous
Youth to the English poets,
Particularly Wordsworth, Marvell
And Chaucer.

I devoted a long and serious
Teaching career to the instruction
Of English girlhood, dealing
Particularly with Shakespeare,
Milton and (of course) Chaucer.

My quieter moments (such of them as
I valued) I devoted
To the Eliot family,
Thomas and George, and (of course)
Chaucer.

So I resent it a little
When new acquaintances say to me –
Oh, an English teacher! How dreadful!
You'll be shocked at my spelling!

I never thought of correcting
Chaucer's.

November in Bristol

On Henbury and Henleaze evening falls.
Homegoing mothers steer gumbooted kids
Past nomad blackcurrants and raspberries,
Wandering roses, trugs, miniature trays
Of succulents, remaindered hyacinths.
Spring shelters here among the plastic pots
And sterile compost, over-wintering
With unsold fireworks, next year's calendars.

These are the dark days. But such solid homes
Semi-detached, bay-windowed, middle-class,
Deter the vagrant rain. The earth's bones ache
Under so much well-pointed masonry;
Each yard is netted, plotted, fenced and wired.
The nomads and the wanderers must learn
Another way of life, and root themselves
Finally in this embittered soil.

The unemployable don't stray out here.
But when I dream of work for them, I see
A Henbury where arms of apple-trees
Encrust gold crumbling walls, and mulberries,
Medlars and quinces grow. Old-fashioned fruits
Aren't choosy; epileptic fingers seem
Quite ordinary to them, while spastic feet
Follow wheelbarrows along worn brick paths.

But not out here. The upright fences guard
Do-it-yourselfers' gardens. Dogs patrol.
No room here for the awkward squad. Their place,
The Remploy Works in Southmead Road, is where
They fit. Gently the winter evening grows
Dark in the empty gardens of Henleaze.

O and M study: the boatman

This employee,
Questioned about working conditions, expressed
No particular dissatisfaction,

Claiming merely
That he had performed the job time out of mind
And was used to it.

We commented
On the lack of proper canteen and toilet
Provision for staff;

On the absence
Of in-service re-training plans; of
Lack of incentive

Or bonus schemes
To achieve higher productivity; on
His monopoly

Of the business,
Which directly conflicts with the findings of
Recent commissions;

And on the fact
That he seems to have worked far beyond the pro-
Per retiring age

Without any
Superannuation arrangements, golden
Handshake, or safeguards

Against redun-
Dancy. Concerning modernisation of
Plant and equipment

We noted that
His boat had been notoriously leaky
For a thousand years

And it was sheer
Luck that there had been no accident so far
In view of the want

Of insurance
Cover. We noted an inappropriate response
At this point, namely

Laughter. We see
Nothing risible in the prospect of loss
Of human life, not

To mention the
Expense and publicity involved. We feel
Alternative modes

Of transport, a
Suspension bridge, or at least a hovercraft
Might be looked into.

Admittedly
This would involve capital investment, and
Higher fares, but since

These have never,
Apparently, been index-linked, we feel some
Rise is overdue.

We are convinced
Time is ripe for a more up to date workforce
Though we must admit

Advertising
In appropriate trade journals has so far
Drawn no candidate.

His own statement was brief:
The after world is unaffected,
He claimed, by inflation,
And he sees himself as simply
One of the facts of death.

Obsessive's Song

Every tick
Of the clock
Dust flies in.

Every tock
Of the clock
Dust must go.

In case dust
Has set foot
In my house

Paint my door
Wash my floor
All night long

Stop the rust
Banish dust
Purify

On a Dead Social Worker

She steered a firm course through equivocal
Currents, and spoke the language of the seas
Though her own dialect was different.
The shipwrecked liked her, hurled their sopping junk
On to her polished planks, and camped on board
Until they swamped the neat craft, and she foundered.

On behalf of Chaos

The trouble with chaos is
Not that it comes again,
But that it keeps on coming and coming and coming,

Like a wave in the sea.
Nothing can hold it back,
It's as inevitable as gravity or time.

But we try to check its
Movement, fight it daily
With Vim and dusters, weed-killer and lawnmowers and

Diaries and hairpins and
Razors and timetables
And railway-lines and overalls and munici-

Pal flowerbeds and banks and
Marriage and weathermen,
Lavatory-paper, papal indices, the law (but

Not the prophets), with verse
And licensing regu-
Lations and bars for music, general elections

And soap. What obsession (Adam's bequest) makes us
So anxious about Chaos? Wouldn't we like it if

It happened? Forests seem
Happier than we are.
Until the Forestry Commission makes them tidy.

Paper friends

He has no message for her.
Meteorological peculiarities and the concerns of
The Drapers' Company in sixteenth-century Shropshire
Hardly constitute a message.

She has no message for him.
Marital problems, and the concerns of
The bees, the bantams and twelve castrated cats
Hardly constitute a message.

If she met him
She would think him a bore.
If he met her
He would think her a witch.

But meeting in the library,
Safely sterilised by history,
He claims her as his path from forgottenness to life;
She claims him as her path from life to forgetting.

Passer-by

The clocks have stopped
Several times before
And *There goes Epikhodov*
We say.

Pigeon-noise in Bath February sunlight,
Turn in a road in the Stour Valley,
Lost child by a fishmonger's slab in Bromley –
He was there.

Only I heard him.

This time
In the moment when you first held me
 – The stopped clocks, the hearts waiting to start –
Before we knew
(And yet we knew it all)
I thought *There goes Epikhodov*

We both heard him.

Phoenix

Around my day work slides its eggshell shape,
Whose spurious logic seems exact as rhyme.
The morning's post is waiting; no escape
From work's irrelevance till coffee-time.
New outpatients; the anxious telephone;
Lists, letters, EEG reports to type.
At one I have an hour when I'm my own,
Then reassume my clerkly stereotype.
This punctuated life fits oddly well.
The things that really count are kept in play;
I lurk contented in my fragile shell,
Knowing that I can break it any day.
Freedom unnerves; servitude sets me free
To hatch the phoenix that I want to be.

Playtime

Behind these railings, on this asphalt ground,
Under the supervision of a qualified adult,
The Iron Age tribe perform their proper rites.

Their names are Darren, Karen, Sharon, their mums
Own microwave ovens, electric coffee-pots.
They study the art of the hopscotch maze.

Their names are Jamie, Jeremy, Hannah, their dads
Drive Volvos and play golf with Japanese.
They pronounce incomprehensible curses and benedictions.

Their brothers are into computing, their sisters
Process words. Solemnly they rehearse
Their fossil cults, initiate novices.

Slaves of the box at home, consuming
Snap-crackle-pop. Here, on the asphalt ground,
They slay, maim, heal, in garbled, earnest games
That need no toy, except the human frame.

Poem for Temps

Pensioned, insured and safe, we are the sheep,
Tucked snugly into permanence. Each year,
We get our bonus and our increment,
Our Shepherd's Christmas speech and Christmas card.
Summer means holidays with pay, a tan
From Spain that will impress the typing pool.
And all the year at discreet intervals
Come the firm's dances at the posh hotel
(For salaried employees), and the odd
Evening at skittles in the local pub
For weekly earners. So we are secure.
We have our places in this special world,
Initials on our teacups; we know where
We ought to sit at meals in the canteen.
We're the elect. The Shepherd knows our names.

You have no obvious horns. You look like us,
Average humanity. But looks deceive.
Your inner horns curve violent and strange.
You come and go, casual and quizzical,
Are unimpressed by our close-hugged routine.
Tangential, underworked and overpaid,
You make us restless, which is wrong for sheep.
So take your horns off to your wilderness,
And, for good measure, take our sins with you.
Our Shepherd loves us; we are permanent.

Problem picture

No doubt about it, it's a very clever picture
Just right for Outpatients. You see,
If you know anything about butterflies,
You can work out what sorts she's put in
(One blue, seven reddish-brown,
And two little tiddlers, not so easy to spot,
Sitting on the buttercup at the bottom).
Alternatively, if you like flowers,
You can puzzle them out for yourself.
There's a poppy, definitely,
And blue vetch, and this buttercup,
And a bit of honeysuckle, and a pink flower
That I don't recognise, and in the middle
What looks like apple-blossom, with a forget-me-not
Growing out of its ear. What you might call
A problem picture, I suppose.

The outpatients love it. First there's the fun
Of identifying the flowers and things,
And when they've done that, they still haven't finished.
It's so lifelike, they say, *it can't be a painting,
Can it? The butterflies must be real
Look at the scales on their wings.*
Then somebody else pipes up, *Well no,
I think you're wrong. This isn't
Painting, it's tapestry. Just look at the texture
Of that stalk.*

Sometimes I contemplate
A notice explaining everything, and adding
This picture was painted by Mrs D Bullock,
Part-time clerk. It is not anything
Special. But then I remember
That patients come to this hospital to be
Puzzled out themselves, and that not anything special
Is exactly what they want to be too.

Rites de passage

Cats aren't adolescent.
No time in their nine lives
When they're not calm,
Infinitely purposeful,
Feline.

They know what to be –
Sleepy, delightful kittens
Next minute, warmly pregnant
Or yodelling round dustbins
For mates.

No embarrassing interregnum
Where they don't know where to put
Their legs, or what to do with
Their sexual urges. Cats
Always know.

How different we make it
For our young, who can't be contented
With shrews, balls of string, or
Milk, and find it so difficult to be
Human.

Rodmell Churchyard

Here the dead are ineradicable,
Caught, like the stubborn church, in unheroic
Attitudes of survival.

Here Mary, Thomas, Emily, John,
Jacob and Rachel lie in sure and certain
Hope of resurrection.

Here economical forefathers found
New uses for the already second-hand.
God's acre a palimpsest

Of these few Sussex names, repetitive
As a stammer. Only she, un-local ghost,
Is so implacably

Not here. Not remembered by the dark church,
Nor by superfluous stones, she who drew us
Here is not here. In the Ouse,

Perhaps, her drenched face floats to chill fish
With its exquisite bones. But here no shred
Speaks of the stateless dead,

Nor thorny corner holds. Only these remains
Doggedly rooting in the holy subsoil
As in life they hugged their holdings,

Wait now for Gabriel. Not she
Whose sphere was the moment, and so
Is duly vaulted in air.

Sexual delinquent

We are all keen to take a look at him.
Women from other departments find excuses
To come into the room
And see what he looks like.
What have we all imagined?
Some hairy hero
Bulging with sex and muscles?
Some sleek seducer,
With an irresistible moustache and
A smooth line in sales talk?
Or even our own boyfriend,
Improved a little, given that keen interest
In women that so few men
Really have?

But all we see
Is a pale, lank-haired pilferer,
Hungry for food, love, anything available,
In charge of a capable spinster.

Sir

A man's word. Women rarely use it.
Term of the servile, grovel towards
Money and power. A forelock-tugger's word.

Jeeves and Dr Johnson only
(Judges of an uncompromising kind)
Transformed *Sir* to an intellectual's snub.

Sir breathes an air of after-dinner port,
Fly-fishing, polo, regimental ties,
Balkan Sobranie, tips, travelling first-class.

If you've a gentle accent, well-cut hair,
If you've a look of I know where I'm going,
Sirs will come flocking like starlings. Slapdash

Shop-assistants, mechanics, waiters, traffic-wardens,
Strangers asking the way, all pay innocent tribute
To the Establishment. And *Sir* can take it.

(It's the woman with her who has to juggle pronouns.)

Song of the flea

My calling is
to study the soft under-belly
of top dogs.

not pedigreed

hounds in ornate kennels, patrons of
well-carved bones

but mongrels who
have made it up the administra-
tive ladder,

whose greed, conceit
and fear it is my calling to
calculate.

I might have been
such a bitch myself, posturing imp-
pressively,

observed with cool
enjoyment by my inferiors.
but I choose

humble angles,
since the perspective of the dust is
accurate.

Swifts

Inland birds are earthbound;
Potter on lawns, squat obstinately
On hot tarmac, loiter under hedges,
Shuffle pigeon-toed along piazzas,
Hang desperate and upside-down on bacon rind,
Pose like debutantes against suitable landscapes –
Anything to avoid the bother of flying.

Only these immigrants are aeronauts,
Spinning their circuits in untroubled air.
Black as magicians, bird's eye view of birds,
A straight line and a curve is all they are.

Their idle ambits trap the invisible
Invisibly. Dark dolphins of the sky,
They mate and eat in their bright element,
And never turn to earth until they die.

T-group

Skinned and absurd, we wriggle in our chairs,
Overgrown embryos, too old and tied
To families, mortgages and careers,
Habitual teaching and habitual thought
To be re-born. The midwife watches us.

Daylight slides past the windows. No one speaks.
We long for our dead children, those past selves
Who never grew, but shrivelled into us.
Compromised and obscured, our silence shrieks
Louder than adult words. The midwife hears.

We know he knows us. X-ray eyed, lynx-eared,
Elephant-nosed, with Geiger-counter mind
He comprehends each blink; our double-glazed
Whitewashed externals mere transparency.
The midwife waits for labour to begin.

One of us speaks. The waters break. Appalled
We watch the foetus flounder, and the red
And brutal hands fish among bloody knots
Forcing fresh air into the stiffened lungs
Of middle age. It will be my turn next.

Forgive me, Merlin. My false pregnancy
Results in nothing but a windy laugh.
I am not brave enough to be re-born.
Your are too kind to be Caesarian.
But cradled in myself I hold in mind
The weird delivery you offered me.

[Group Therapy, on a psychology course. This poem was written in 1970,
before she actually 'became a poet'. RVB]

The bowl of roses

Presents, like prophecies, are self-willed.
Intent on integrity, they materialise
In enigmas. Here's your design:
Potpourri cottage, publisher waiting,
And on the desk, flanking the bowl of roses,
The trim tower of paper, the shaggy other,
Down which a masterpiece dances,
My hands commuting between.

I can get there by candlelight.

Here, on a different front,
Three grey sisters, toothless, in hats,
Wait to be taken home to Withywood;
Here the deluded tell the view from their eyes
In the halting exact language of the sane;
Here people turn into cabbages (look,
No wand!) and cabbages stare
From human wounded faces.

I can get there by candlelight;
I can get here only by coming.

So wishes come true, but we're too rational
To recognise them. Each day begins
And ends with you, a perfect circle.
Can you not see that this is my bowl of roses?

I can get there by candlelight.

The brides of Christ

The brides of Christ
  Learn their fierce Lover by degrees.
The postulants, enticed
  But doubtful of their power to please,
Spend six months in the suburbs of his grace,
  Then, veiled in white,
As novices, peruse the Husband's face.
  The public rite
(High-heeled and lurching, awkwardly mundane)
  Brands them as his, with scapular and ring.
They pledge a life-intention, but remain
  Not fully His until the fastening
Of life-profession, judged and ratified
By all the sisterhood. The noose is tied.

The brides of men
  Follow the rituals of their sort.
Go courting, wonder when;
  And how, and who; decide they ought,
Then take the public steps: announce
  Their day, choose, calculate, receive,
Find priest or registrar who will pronounce
  A public formula which few believe;
Then photographed, confetti'd, leave the cake
  For seasoned bridesmaids, practice man-and-wife
For seven hard days' honeymoon, then take
  Their marriage status into daily life.
At tea-breaks trail the album round to prove
They're qualified practitioners of love.

For you and me, no rite
  Is proper. Church and state
Afford no precedent for us to cite.
  No customary feasts inaugurate
A double life. No dear regalia –

Bouquet, ring, top hat – seems appropriate
So love extemporises Bacchanalia
    To suit its gaily unofficial state.
Then may the feast be permanent; may all
    The world itself become our wedding guest
Since no date's ours, the year perpetual
    Be anniversary for the unblest.

They need no ring of bells, licensed embraces,
Who wear their daily joy upon their faces.

The golden girls

The golden girls whom no one ever saves,
Bright cannon-fodder, poppied, delicate,
Step lightly to their cattle-trucks.

Sacrifice hums in their enchanted hair,
Anointed fingers uncurl to embrace
The waiting genocide.

Fresh-eyed, bright-brained and blackbird-voiced, they dance,
Not knowing where they are, along the rim
Of No-man's-land.

O golden girls, why did you let your fathers
Summon the cattle-truck? Why did you choose
The genocides? Why did you help them dig
Your graves?

The head housemaid tells the receptionist a joke

Enters office intent-eyed.
Has something for me. Not gift.

> *Did you hear the one about the two tortoises?*

Is about-to-tell-me-a-joke.
I am a-person-about-to-receive-a-joke.
Men or tortoise? I watch.

> *The wife said to the husband: Look, I'm running out of*
> *sugar, butter, marge. It's time you went down to the super-*
> *market for me. So old man tortoise went off.*

Eyes for cues.
Eyes are brown,
And move. Rest: hold still
In case jokes spills. Listen!
Tortoise. Remember.
(Pause)

Concentrate. Watch.

> *Well, spring passed. Summer passed, autumn passed, winter*
> *passed, and she began to think something's happened to him,*
> *he's not coming back. So she went to the front door, opened*
> *it, and there he was, about twenty yards away.*

Serious and beautiful.
She rehearses a joke like
A sugared sonnet. I stand
Upright as a guardsman, a vase
To receive her offering. Must not
Fail.
(Pause)

> *So she shouted to him: hurry up slowcoach! I'm waiting for*
> *all that stuff.*

Is this
The promised end? I should have laughed?
No. My image still
In her moving eyes. Joke holds.

(Pause)
And he said if you don't shut up I won't go.

I laugh. Relief. I understood.
She laughs. Triumphant laugh of the creator.
It's all right. We both laugh.
We made it together.

The Receptionist

I'm the receptionist. I am an ear
That listens on the phone, a hand that makes
Appointments in the book, a pair of feet
To fetch you what you need. I am a room
Where you can pick and poke and use my phone,
My scissors and my paper. I am nothing.
I listen and I mark, but to no end.
Mistakes are mine, but nothing that's well done
By me is ever noticed. To be nothing
Has its own consolations. Mostly I am happy
But sometimes ear and hand and willing feet
And empty room know they are all one body
And intermesh. And I am Cerberus,
Guardian of Hell. Beware of me. I bite.

This quiet little Welshwoman

This quiet little Welshwoman,
Unremarkable in Cwmbran
In her pink nylon overall
And her harmless face,
Looks out of the window,
Endlessly stroking her wrists.

I don't know what fantasies
Flower in her unremarkable
Mind under the overall
And the pink face.
From the shelter of my sanity
I watch, appalled, as
She looks out of the window,
Endlessly stroking her wrists.

To the Holy Ghost

(after talking to a Benedictine monk about women)

I like to think that you're a woman
    In all that heavenly world of men.
You'd understand what we are feeling
    And speak up for us now and then.

It's hard for God to be a woman
    Surrounded as He has to be
By Thrones and Powers and Dominations,
    All strong in masculinity;

By Seraphs, Cherubs and Archangels,
    All burning upwards, fiercely male;
By Saints and Abbots and Archbishops –
    Holy, of course, but wholly male.

I wouldn't want to think of Heaven
    Capitulating to my cry,
Becoming a celestial teashop,
    Or saintlier W. I.

But when the Male Voice Choirs cease to thunder,
    And when the Son has spoken, your turn's next;
Put in a kindly word (or piece of birdsong)
    For our un-Godly sex.

Typist

She sitteth among the cymbals.
She clasheth the loud cymbals.

Men's faded voices twitter
Their dreams in her brusque ears.
Automatically she corrects their grammar.

Her drawer holds bright sharp things
That cut, punch, prick, impale.
She has a deadly way with a knife.
She can kill paper.

She sitteth among the cymbals.

Mistress of words,
She summons voices from the world's end
With one finger.

Benighted in the glacier of their scorn,
Her masters' jolly grins
Freeze their cheekbones.

She clasheth the loud cymbals.

One day she will speak her mind
In perfect grammar. One day she will snip
Their tapes with her scissor.

One day she will rise with all her sisters
Their war cry will be QWERTYUIOP.
They will kill men.

She sitteth among the cymbals.
She clasheth the loud cymbals.

Wise children

Adam's lot count
And classify
And know where the
Breadknife is.

Aristotle
Was one of us.
He organised
Reasoning and

Zoology. Arts
And syllogisms
Sprang briskly to
Their proper places.

Linnaeus with
Cold Swedish eyes
Saw the untidy
World of flora

And fauna and
Called them all to
Order. Adam
In Paradise

Did no better.
I in my own
Kitchen emulate
All of them.

Teacups know their
Places, plates have
Strict order of
Precedence and

Glasses of each
Sort are strictly
Segregated.
But Eve's children

See how many
Lovely worlds lie
Hidden in each
Apple, and would

Never dream of
Counting the pips.

Woman's world

They inhabit other
Worlds, these browsers
At the rack of magazines.

The gardener, the yachtsman
Adrift in a world of tackle
And climbing begonias.

Their fingers move on the thick paper
They are already there, in
The Channel, the bastard trench.

The cavey-breeder
Sees it all before him
The impossible triumphs calmly achieved at shows
Before he has even bought his magazine
Let alone a guinea-pig

Only the women fail
To enter this golden arena
Of dedicated action

Their magazines offer
Not the single track of *Amateur
Gardening, Motorboat
And Yachting, Pet-fancier's Gazette*,

Only the impossible junctions
Of being woman.

Writer's garden

Benign the cedar broods. The little owls
And squirrels patronise its scented boughs.
The gentle garden dips into the stream,
Fishing rights, landing stage. The honeyed walls,
Fur-coated hedges are not needed here
As boundaries, but modulate the change
From one elegant sector to the rest.

Imagination keeps them all afloat,
The squirrels and the owls, the cedar tree,
Yew hedges, fishing rights. Their lives depend
On his frail skull, his white-skinned hand. He writes

And millions read. His thorny, skyless world
Of raincoats, bureaucrats and cups of tea,
Forged love, false passports, seedy foreign cars,
Secures the gold that animates this green.
Film rights support the fishing; serialised,
The cedar's steady for a year or two.
His paperbacks cover suburbia.

Briefly the frail skull and the white-skinned hand
Survey the sunlight. In his study now
He digs for gold. The squirrels can't see him.
Snaps of suburban gardens line the walls.